CW00418482

Because you are but a young man, beware of temptations and snares; and above all, be careful to keep yourself in the use of means; resort to good company; and howbeit you be nicknamed a Puritan, and mocked, yet care not for that, but rejoice and be glad, that they who are scorned and scoffed by this godless and vain world, and nicknamed Puritans, would admit you to their society; for I must tell you, when I am at this point as you see me, I get no comfort to my soul by any second means under heaven but from those who are nicknamed Puritans. They are the men that can give a word of comfort to a wearied soul in due season, and that I have found by experience . . .

THE LAST AND HEAVENLY SPEECHES, AND
GLORIOUS DEPARTURE, OF JOHN, VISCOUNT KENMURE

CHRIST IS BEST;

OR,

ST PAUL'S STRAIT

Richard Sibbes

For I am in a strait between two, having a desire to depart, and to be with Christ, which is best of all; nevertheless, to abide in the flesh is most needful for you (Phil. 1:23, 24).

THE BANNER OF TRUTH TRUST

THE BANNER OF TRUTH TRUST
3 Murrayfield Road, Edinburgh EH12 6EL, UK
P.O. Box 621, Carlisle, PA 17013, USA

*

© Banner of Truth Trust 2012

ISBN: 978 1 84871 057 3

*

Typeset in 10.5 / 13.5 pt Adobe Caslon Pro
at the Banner of Truth Trust, Edinburgh

Printed in the USA by
Versa Press, Inc.,
East Peoria, IL

Taken from *Christ is Best* in
The Works of Richard Sibbes
(Edinburgh: Banner of Truth, repr. 2001),
vol. 1, pp. 335-50.

The original text has been lightly edited to
modernize archaic pronouns and verb forms.

CONTENTS

FOREWORD

IF your Christian life has become at all stale and joyless, then a tonic I heartily recommend is this most cheery Puritan, Richard Sibbes (1577-1635). Really, anything of his will do, but this little work will give you a fine taste.

Christ is Best was originally a funeral sermon preached by Sibbes, opening up Paul's dilemma (in *Phil.* 1:23, 24): would he rather die and be with Christ, which is best of all, or live on so as to build up the church further? Through it, Sibbes displays how beautifully different a lively faith is from dead religion. In dead religion, one can easily talk of receiving 'grace' so as to 'get heaven'. Paul does not. Instead of desiring to depart and be *in heaven*, Paul says he desires to depart and be *with Christ*. For, says Sibbes, 'heaven is not heaven without Christ.' In other words, true faith is not about buying into some abstract system of salvation (even one paid for by Christ); first and foremost it is about the Spirit bringing me to know, love, and desire Christ himself.

Knowing that made all the difference to what Sibbes was about as a pastor and preacher. Wanting more than upright behaviour, more than mere assent to gospel truth, Sibbes sought to cultivate in his listeners such holy *desires* as Paul had.

'Desires are the immediate issue of the soul', he said; in fact, 'Nothing characterises a Christian so much as holy and blessed desires, for there is no hypocrisy in them.' Paul had been brought to appreciate that Christ truly is best, that he is better and more desirable than anything else in life or death: Sibbes simply wanted our hearts to beat with Paul's.

But how? How can we—we who naturally find almost anything but God alluring—have our hearts and their desires so redirected? How can we, without hypocrisy, come to embrace Christ as our most dearly cherished treasure? Sibbes explains how it was for Paul:

St Paul loved the person of Christ, because he felt sweet experience that Christ loved him; his love was but a reflection of Christ's love first. He loved to see Christ, to embrace him, and enjoy him that had done so much and suffered so much for his soul, that had forgiven him so many sins, *etc.* (pp. 11, 12, below)

In other words, hearts begin to desire Christ above all when they sense how much he loves us sinners, how much he has suffered for our forgiveness, how unfathomably kind and merciful he is and has been. We love him, because he first loved us (*1 John* 4:19).

Sibbes knew well that when hearts are thus captivated by Christ and turned to delight in him above all, something happens. He put it like this: 'Beloved, those that have warmed their hearts at the fire of God's love, they think zeal itself to be coldness, and fruitfulness to be barrenness. Love is a boundless affection.' What all my efforts could not achieve, the love of Christ achieves: it wins me to love God and love others with sincerity, freedom, and spontaneity; I begin to *enjoy* holiness and *hate* sin.

Sibbes's preaching awoke and invigorated faith, love and joy in Christ for great numbers in his own day. I pray now for you, reader, that this little sermon may cause you to say 'Christ really is best of all; he is my highest desire and my only boast.'

MICHAEL REEVES
Oxford
February 2012

CHRIST IS BEST;

OR,

ST PAUL'S STRAIT.[1]

For I am in a strait between two, having a desire to depart, and to be with Christ, which is best of all; nevertheless, to abide in the flesh is most needful for you.

Philippians 1:23, 24

THE Apostle Paul here, had a double desire, one in regard of himself, to be with Christ; another, out of his love of God's church and people, to abide still in the flesh;

---

[1] A sermon preached at the funeral of Mr Christopher Sherland (1593-1632), late Recorder of Northampton.

and between these two he is in a great strait, not knowing which to choose. But the love of the church of Christ triumphed in him, above the love of his own salvation, so as he was content, out of self-denial, to lack the joys of heaven for a time, that he might yet further comfort the people of God.

In the words you have,

1. *St Paul's straits*;

2. His *desires* that caused them, as in regard of himself, which was to be with Christ; so, in respect of the church of God, which was *to abide still here*;

3. The reasons of both, (i) to *be with Christ* is far better for me, (ii) to *abide in the flesh,* more needful for you; and

4. His resolution upon all, being willing for the church's good *still to abide here*, rather than go to heaven and enjoy his own happiness.

St Paul's soul was as a ship, between two winds, tossed up and down, and as iron between two lodestones, drawn first one way, then another; the one lodestone was his own good, to be in heaven; the other was the good of God's people, to abide still in the flesh.

Obs. Observe hence *that the servants of God are oftentimes in great straits.*

Some things are so exceeding bad that, without any deliberation or delay at all, we ought presently to abominate them, as Satan's temptations to sin, to distrust, despair, *etc.* Some things also are so good that we should immediately cleave unto them, as matters of religion and piety. There should be no delay in these holy businesses. Deliberation here, argues weakness. Some things, again, are of an ambiguous and doubtful nature, requiring our best consideration. Such was Paul's strait in this place. He had reasons swaying him on both sides; and such is the happy estate of a Christian, that whatsoever he had chosen had been well for him; only, God who rules our judgments, will have us to make choice. God might have determined whether Paul should live or die, but he would not without Paul's choice. That which is good, is not good to us, but upon choice and advice. When God has given us abilities to discourse and examine things, he will have us make use of them, and therefore the apostle uses reasons on both sides, it is better to die for me, it is better to live for you, *etc*.

Wicked men have their deliberations, and their straits too; but it is with the rich man in the gospel, what they shall do, how they may pull down their barns, and build bigger, *etc*. (*Luke* 12:18). Their main strait is at the hour of death; live they cannot, die they dare not. There is so much guilt of sin upon their consciences, they know not which way to turn themselves. Oh, what fearful straits will sin bring men into! But the apostle was straitened in an higher nature than this, whether it were better for the glory of God (which he aimed at above all) for him to go to heaven and enjoy happiness in his own person, or to abide still, for the comfort of God's saints, on earth.

The ground of this difficulty and strait was his present desire. *I have a desire*. Desires are the immediate issue of the soul, the motion and stirring of the same to something that likes it. When there is anything set before the soul having a magnetical force, as the lodestone, to draw out the motions thereof, we call that desire, though for the present it enjoys it not.

1. St Paul's desire was, *spiritual*; not after happiness, so much as holiness. 'O miserable man that I am', says he, 'who shall deliver me from this body of death?' (*Rom.* 7:24). His desire of death was to be freed from the *body of sin*, more than to be taken out of the flesh; and his desire of holiness, to have Christ's image stamped on his soul, was more than of eternal happiness. Nature cannot do this. It is a work above the flesh, for that will not hear of departing, but rather bids God and Christ depart from it.

2. This desire came from a *taste of sweetness in communion with Christ*; and those desires that most ravish the soul in apprehension of heavenly things are ever the most holy. St Paul knew what a sweet communion Christ was.

3. It was a *constant* desire. He does not say I desire, but I have a desire, I carry the

same about me, and that carries me to a love of Christ and his members.

4. It was *efficacious*, not a naked velleity,[2] not a wish of the sluggard, I would, and I would, but a strong desire, carrying him even through death itself to Christ. Desires thus qualified are blessed desires. As where we see vapours arise, there are springs usually below them, so where these desires are, there is always a spring of grace in that soul. Nothing characterises a Christian so much as holy and blessed desires, for there is no hypocrisy in them.

I desire to depart. There must be a *parting* and a departing; there must be a parting in this world with all outward excellencies, from the sweet enjoyment of the creatures; there must be a parting between soul and

---

[2] Mere inclination.

body, between friend and friend, and whatever is near and dear unto us. All shall determine in death.

And there must be a *departing* also. Here we cannot stay long; away we must; we are for another place. Oh that we could make use of these common truths! How far are we from making a right use of the mysteries of salvation, when we cannot make use of common truths which we have daily experience of! Holy Moses, considering the suddenness of his departure hence, begged of God to teach him to number his days, that he might apply his heart unto wisdom, (*Psa.* 90:12).

Death is but a departing; which word is taken from loosing from the shore, or removing of a ship to another coast.[3] We

---

[3] 'Death is but a *departing* . . . which word is taken from

must all be unloosened from our houses of clay, and be carried to another place, to heaven. Paul labours to sweeten so harsh a thing as death, by comfortable expressions of it. It is but a sleep, a going home, a laying aside our earthly tabernacle, to teach us this point of heavenly wisdom, that we should look on death as it is now in the gospel, not as it was in the law and by nature; for so it is a passage to hell, and lets us in to all miseries whatsoever.

Some things are desirable for themselves, as happiness and holiness; some things are desirable not for themselves, but as they make way to better things, being sour, and bitter to nature themselves; as medicine is desired not for itself, but for

---

loosing from the shore, or removing of a ship to another coast' (see *Luke* 8:38, and *2 Tim.* 4:6, and *Phil.* 1:23, all in the Greek).

health. We desire health for itself, and medicine for health, *so to be with Christ* is a thing desirable of itself; but because we cannot come to Christ but by the dark passage of death, says Paul, *I desire to depart*, that so my death may be a passage to Christ; so that death was the object of St Paul's desire so far as it made way for better things.

I desire to depart, and to be with Christ.

To be with Christ that came from heaven to be here on earth with us, and descended that we should ascend; to be with him, who has done and suffered so much for us; to be with Christ who delighted to be with us; to be with Christ who emptied himself, and became of no reputation, who became poor to make us rich; to be with Christ our husband, now contracted here; that all may be made up in heaven; this was the thing Paul desired.

Quest. Why does he not say, I desire to be in heaven?

Ans. Because heaven is not heaven without Christ. It is better to be in any place with Christ than to be in heaven itself without him. All delicacies without Christ are but as a funeral banquet. Where the master of the feast is away, there is nothing but solemnness. What is all without Christ? I say the joys of heaven are not the joys of heaven without Christ; he is the very heaven of heaven.

True love is carried to the person. It is adulterous love, to love the thing, or the gift, more than the person. St Paul loved the person of Christ, because he felt sweet experience that Christ loved him; his love was but a reflection of Christ's love first. He loved to see Christ, to embrace him, and enjoy him who had done so much and suffered so much for his soul, who had forgiven him so many sins, *etc.*

The reason is, because it is best of all. To be with Christ is to be at the spring-head of all happiness. It is to be in our proper element. Every creature thinks itself best in its own element, that is the place it thrives in, and enjoys its happiness in; now Christ is the element of a Christian.

Again, it is far better, because to be with Christ is to have the marriage consummate. Is not marriage better than the contract? Is not home better than absence? To be with Christ is to be at home. Is not triumph better than to be in conflict? But to be with Christ is to triumph over all enemies, to be out of Satan's reach. Is not perfection better than imperfection? Here all is but imperfect, in heaven there is perfection; therefore that is much better than any good below, for all are but shadows here, *there* is reality. What are riches? What are the worm-eaten pleasures of the world? What are the honours of the earth, but mere shadows of good? 'At the right hand of Christ are pleasures indeed' (*Psa.* 16:11), honours indeed, riches indeed; *there* is reality.

If we speak of grace, and good things, it is better to be with Christ than enjoy the graces and comforts of the Holy Spirit here. Why? Because they are all stained and mixed. Here our peace is interrupted with desertion and trouble. Here the joys of the Holy Spirit are mingled with sorrow. Here the grace in a man is with combat of flesh and spirit, but in heaven there is pure peace, pure joy, pure grace: for what is glory but the perfection of grace? Grace indeed is glory here, but it is glory with conflict. The Scripture calls grace glory sometimes, but it is glory with imperfection. Beloved, perfection is better than imperfection, therefore to be with Christ is far better.

And is it much 'far better' to die, that we may be with Christ, than to live here a conflicting life? Why should we then fear death, which is but a passage to Christ? It is but a grim sergeant that lets us into a glorious palace, that strikes off our bolts, that takes off our rags, that we may be clothed with better robes, that ends all our misery, and is the beginning of all our happiness. Why should we therefore be afraid of death? It is but a departure to a better condition? It is but as Jordan to the children of Israel, by which they passed to Canaan. It is but as the Red Sea by which they were going that way. Therefore we have no reason to fear death. Of itself it is an enemy indeed, but now it is harmless, nay, now it is become a friend, amicable to us, a sweet friend. It is one part of the church's jointure,[4] death. ' All things are yours', says the Apostle, Paul and Apollos, 'life and death' (*1 Cor.* 3:22). Death is ours and for our good. It does us more good than all the friends we have in the world. It determines and ends all our misery and sin; and it is the suburbs of heaven. It lets us into those joys above. It is a shame for Christians therefore, to be afraid of that that Paul here makes the object of his desire.

But may not a good Christian fear death?

I answer, Not, so far as a Christian is led with the Spirit of God, and is truly spiritual; for the Spirit carries us upward. But as far as we are earthly and carnal, and biased

---

[4] Property settled upon a woman at marriage to be enjoyed after her husband's death.

downward to things below, we are loath to depart hence. In some cases God's children are afraid to die, because their accounts are not ready. Though they love Christ, and are in a good way, yet notwithstanding, because they have not prepared themselves by care, as a woman that has her husband abroad and desires his coming, but all is not prepared in the house, therefore she desires that he may stay awhile; so the soul that is not exact, that is not in that frame that it should be in, says, 'Oh stay a while that I may recover my strength, before I go hence and be no more seen' (*Psa.* 39:13); but as far as we are guided by the Spirit of God sanctifying us, and are in such a condition as we should be in, so far the thoughts of death ought not to be terrible to us; nor indeed are they.

Beloved, there is none but a Christian that can desire death; because it is the end of all comfort here, it is the end of all callings and employments, of all sweetness whatsoever in this world. If another man that is not a Christian, desire heaven, he desires it not as heaven, or to be with Christ as Christ; he desires it under some notion suitable to his corruption; for our desires are as ourselves are, as our aims are. No carnal worldly man, but has carnal worldly aims. A worldly man cannot go beyond the world. It is his sphere. A carnal man cannot go beyond the flesh. Therefore a carnal man cannot desire heaven. A man that is under the power of any lust, can desire nothing but the satisfying of that lust. Heaven is no place for such. None but a child of God can desire that; for if we consider heaven, and *to be with Christ*, to be *perfect holiness*, can he desire it that hates holiness here? Can he desire the image of God upon him that hates it in others and in himself too? Can he desire the communion of saints that of all societies hates it the most? Can he desire to be free from sin, that engulfs himself continually in sin? He cannot, and therefore as long as he is under the thraldom and dominion of any lust he may desire heaven indeed, but it is only so far as he may have his lusts there, his pleasures, honours, and riches there too. If he may have heaven with that, he is contented; but alas! brethren, heaven must not be so desired. St Paul did otherwise; he desired *to be dissolved; to be with Christ*. He desired it as the perfection of the image of God, under the notion of holiness and freedom from sin, as I said before.

Which is far better.

Obs. Again, we see that *God reserves the best for the last.*[5] God's last works are his best works. The new heaven and the new earth are the best; the second wine that Christ created himself was the best; spiritual things are better than natural. A Christian's last is his best.

God will have it so, for the comfort of Christians, that every day they live, they may think, my best is behind, my best is to come, that every day they rise, they may think, I am nearer heaven one day than I was before, I am nearer death, and therefore nearer to Christ. What a solace is this to a

---

[5] 'God reserves the best for the last.' This more than once repeated saying of Sibbes, probably suggested to Thomas Brooks the titles of two of his minor writings, *A String of Pearls; or the Best Things Reserved till Last* (1657); *A Believer's Last Day is his Best Day* (1651).

gracious heart! A Christian is a happy man in his life, but happier in his death, because then he goes to Christ; but happiest of all in heaven, for then he is *with Christ*. How contrary to a carnal man, that loves according to the sway of his own base lusts! He is miserable in his life, more miserable in his death, but most miserable of all after death. I beseech you, lay this to heart. I think, considering that death is but a way for us to be with Christ, *which is far better*, this should sweeten the thinking of death to us, and we should comfort ourselves daily that we are nearer happiness.

Quest. But how shall we attain this sanctified sweet desire that Paul had, to die, and be with Christ?

Ans. 1. *Let us carry ourselves as Paul did*, and then we shall have the same desires. St Paul, before death, in his lifetime, 'had his conversation in heaven' (*Phil.* 3:20). His mind was there, and his soul followed after. There is no man's soul comes into heaven but his mind is there first. It was an easy matter for him to desire to be with Christ, having his conversation in heaven already. Paul in meditation was where he was not and he was not where he was. He was in heaven when his body was on earth.

2. Again, *St Paul had loosed his affections from all earthly things*; therefore it was an easy matter for him to desire to be with Christ. 'I am crucified to the world, and the world is crucified to me' *etc.* (*Gal.* 6:14). If once a Christian comes to this pass, death will be welcome to him. Those whose hearts are fastened to the world cannot easily desire Christ.

3. Again, *holy St Paul laboured to keep a good conscience in all things*. 'Herein I exercise

myself, to have a good conscience towards God and men', *etc.* (*Acts* 24:16). It is easy for him to desire to be dissolved, that has his conscience *sprinkled with the blood of Christ* (*Heb.* 10:22), free from a purpose of living in any sin. But where there is a stained, defiled, polluted conscience, there cannot be this desire; for the heart of man, naturally, as the prophet says, 'casts up mire and dirt' (*Isa.* 57:20). It casts up fears, and objections, and murmurings, and repinings. Oh, beloved, we think not what mischief sin will do us, when we suffer it to seize upon our consciences; when it is once written there with the *claw of a diamond and with a pen of iron* (*Jer.* 17:1), who shall get it out? Nothing but great repentance and faith, applying the blood of Christ. It is no easy matter to get it off there, and to get the conscience at peace again; and when conscience is not appeased, there will be all clamours within. It will fear to appear before the judgment seat. A guilty conscience trembles at the mention of death. Therefore I wonder how men that live in swearing, in looseness, in filthiness, in deboisedness[6] of life, that labour to satisfy their lusts and corruptions, I wonder how they can think of death without trembling, considering that they are under the guilt of so many sins. Oh, beloved, the exercising of the heart to keep a clear conscience, can only breed this desire in us to depart, and to be with Christ. You have a company of wretched persons, proud enough in their own conceits, and censorious. Nothing can please them whose whole life is acted by Satan joining with the lusts of their flesh, and they do nothing but

---

[6] That is, 'debauchery'.

put stings into death every day, and arm death against themselves, which when once it appears, their conscience, which is a hell within them, is wakened, and where are they? They can stay here no longer; they must appear before the dreadful Judge; and then where are all their pleasures and contentments, for which they neglected heaven and happiness, peace of conscience, and all? Oh, therefore let us walk holily with our God, and maintain inward peace all we can, if we desire to depart hence with comfort.

4. Again, *Paul had got assurance that he was in Christ, by his union with him.* 'I live not', says he, 'but Christ liveth in me' (*Gal.* 2:20). Therefore labour for assurance of salvation, that you may feel the Spirit of Christ in you, sanctifying and altering your carnal dispositions to be like his. 'I know whom I have trusted' (*2 Tim.* 1:12), says

he. He was as sure of his salvation, as if he had had it already. How few live as if they intended any such matter as this—assurance of salvation—without which how can we ever desire to be dissolved, and to be with Christ? Will a man leave his house, though it be never so mean, when he knows not whither to go? Will a man leave the prison, when he knows he shall be carried to execution? Oh, no; he had rather be in the dungeon still. So when there is guilt on the soul, that it is not assured of salvation, but rather has cause to fear the contrary, can it say, 'I desire to depart, and be with Christ' *etc.*? No; they had rather abide in the flesh still, if they could, for ever, for all eternity. Therefore, if we would come to Paul's desire, labour to come to the frame of the holy apostle's spirit. He knew whom he had believed; he was assured that nothing could separate him from the love of God, neither life, nor death, nor anything whatsoever that could befall him (*Rom.* 8:38, 39).

5. *Paul had an art of sweetening the thoughts of death.* He considered it only as a departure from earth to heaven. When death was presented unto him as a passage to Christ, it was an easy matter to desire the same; therefore it should be the art of Christians to present death as a passage to a better life, to labour to bring our souls into such a condition, as to think death not to be a death to us, but the death of itself. Death dies when I die, and I begin to live when I die. It is a sweet passage to life. We never live till we die. This was Paul's art. He had a care to look beyond death to heaven; and when he looked upon death, he looked on it but as a passage to Christ: so let it be our art and skill. Would we cherish a desire

to die, let us look on death as a passage to Christ, and look beyond it to heaven. All of us must go through this dark passage to Christ,[7] which when we consider as Paul did, it will be an easy matter to die.

I come now to the next words—*Nevertheless, to abide in the flesh is more needful for you.*

This is the other desire of Paul, that brought him into this strait. He was troubled whether he should die, which was far better for himself, or live, which

---

[7] 'All of us must go through this dark passage to Christ.' Sir William Davenant has finely used this saying—

> 'O harmless Death! whom still the valiant brave,
> The wise expect, the sorrowful invite,
> And all the good embrace, *who know the grave*
> *A short dark passage to eternal light.*'

Longfellow has the same thought:

> 'The grave is but a cover'd bridge, leading from light
> To light, *through a brief darkness.*'

was more needful for them; but the love of God's people did prevail in holy St Paul, above the desire of heaven, and the present enjoying his own happiness. Oh, the power of grace in the hearts of God's children, that makes them content to be without the joys of heaven for a time, that they may do God's service, in serving his church here upon earth.

Obs. 1. Observe hence, *that the lives of worthy men, especially magistrates and ministers, are very needful for the church of God.*

The reason is, because God's manner of dispensation is to convey all good to men by the means of men like ourselves for the most part; and this he does to knit us into a holy communion one with another. Therefore it is needful that holy men should abide. In regard of the church of God their lives are very useful.

If we consider good, the great benefit that comes by them, we shall easily yield to this; for what a deal of sin does a good magistrate stop and hinder! When there were good judges and good kings in Israel, see what a reformation there was. Antichrist could not come in when the Roman empire flourished (*2 Thess.* 2:7), though now the Roman empire hinder the fall of antichrist, because antichrist has given her the cup of fornication and they are drunk with the whore's cup; but at the first it was not so. Beloved, whilst good magistrates and good ministers continue in a place, there is a hindrance of heresies and sin, *etc.* If they be once removed, there is a floodgate opened for all manner of sin and corruption to break in at. Yea, there is abundance of good comes in by gracious persons.

Christ is Best 29

1. By their *counsel and direction*; 'The lips of the righteous feed many' (*Prov.* 10:21).

2. By their *reformation of abuses, by planting God's ordinances and good orders*, whereby God's wrath is appeased. They stand in the gap, and stop evil. They reform it, and labour to establish that which is pleasing to God.

3. Gracious persons, in what condition soever they are, *carry the blessing of God with them*. Wheresoever they are, God and his blessing goes along with them.

4. They do a great deal of good *by their pattern and example*. 'They are the lights of the world' (*Phil.* 2:15), that give aim to others in the darkness of this life.

5. They can by their *prayers bind God*, as it were, *that he shall not inflict his judgments*. They do a world of good by this way. A praying force and army is as good as a fighting

army. Moses did as much good by prayer as the soldiers in the valley when they fought with Amalek. They are favourites with God in heaven, therefore St Paul says, *It is needful for you that I abide in the flesh.* Gracious men are public treasures, and storehouses, wherein every man has a share, a portion; they are public springs in the wilderness of this world, to refresh the souls of people; they are trees of righteousness, that stretch out their boughs for others to shelter under and to gather fruit from. You have an excellent picture of this in Daniel, in the dream of Nebuchadnezzar (*Dan.* 4:21). The magistrates there, are compared to a great tree, wherein the birds build their nests and the beasts shelter themselves; so a good magistrate, especially if he be in great place, is as a great tree for comfort and shelter. Oh, beloved, the lives of good men are very useful. A good man, says the philosopher, is a common good; because as soon as ever a man becomes gracious, he has a public mind, as he has a public place, nay, whether he has a public place or no, he has a public mind. It is needful, therefore, that there be such men alive.

If this be so, then we may lament the death of worthy men, because we lose part of our strength in the loss of such, God's custom being to convey much good by them; and when there is scarcity of good men, we should say with Micah, 'Woe is me, the good is perished from the earth' (*Mic.* 7:2). They keep judgments from a place, and derive a blessing upon it. Howsoever the world judges them, and accounts them not worthy to live, yet God accounts the world unworthy of them. They are God's jewels, they are his treasure and his portion, therefore we ought to lament their death, and to desire their lives; and we ought to desire our own lives, as long as we may be useful to the church; and be content to want heaven for a time. Beloved, it is not for the good of God's children that they live; as soon as ever they are in the state of grace they have a title to heaven, but it is for others. When once we are in Christ, we live for others, not for ourselves. That a father is kept alive, it is for his children's sake; that good magistrates are kept alive, it is for their subjects' sake; that a good minister is kept alive, out of the present enjoying of heaven, it is for the people's sake that God has committed to him to instruct; for, as Paul says here, in regard of my own particular, *it is better for me to be with Christ.*

Use. If God convey so much good by worthy men to us, then what wretches are they that malign them, persecute them, *etc.*, speak ill of those that speak to God for them? Does the world continue for a company of wretches, a company of profane, blasphemous, loose, disorderly livers? Oh no; for if God had not a church in the world, a company of good people, heaven and earth would fall in pieces. There would be an end presently. It is for good people only that the world continues. They are the pillars of the tottering world, they are the stakes in the fence, they are the foundation of the building, and if they were once taken out, all would come down; there would be a confusion of all. Therefore those that oppose and disquiet gracious and good men are enemies to their own good; they cut the bough which they stand on; they labour to pull down the house that covers themselves, being blinded with malice and a diabolical spirit. Take heed of such a disposition. It comes near to the sin against the Holy Ghost to hate any man for goodness; because, perhaps, his good life reproaches us. Such a one would hate Christ himself if he were here. How can a man desire to be with Christ when he hates his image in another? Therefore if God convey so much good by other men that are good, let us make much of them, as public persons, as instruments of our good. Take away malice, and pride, and a poisonful spirit, and all their good is ours. What hinders that we have no good by them? Pride and an envious spirit, *etc.*

Obs. A second thing that I observe hence is this, *holy and gracious men, that are led by the Spirit of God, can deny themselves and their own best good for the church's benefit.* They know that God has appointed them as instruments to convey good to others; and knowing, this, they labour to come to Paul's spirit here, to desire to live, to have life in patience, and death in desire in regard of themselves; for it were much better for a good man to be in heaven, out of misery, out of this conflicting condition with the devil and devilish-minded men.

Reason 1. The reason is, because a good man, as soon as he is a good man, *has the spirit of love in him*, and love 'seeketh not her own' (*1 Cor.* 13:5), but the good of another; and as the love of Christ and the love of God possesses and seizes upon the soul, so self-love decays. What is gracious love but a decay of self-love? The more self-love decays, the more we deny ourselves.

2. Again, God's people have the *Spirit of Christ in them*, who minded not his own

things (*1 Cor.* 10:24). If Christ had minded his own things, where had our salvation been? Christ was content to leave heaven, and to take our nature upon him, to be Emmanuel, God with us, that we might be with God for ever in heaven. He was content, not only to leave heaven, but to be born in the womb of a virgin. He was content to stoop to the grave. He stooped as low as hell in love to us. Now, where Christ's Spirit is, it will bring men from their altitudes and excellencies, and make them to stoop to serve the church, and account it an honour to be an instrument to do good. Christ was content to be accounted, not only a servant of God, but of the church. 'My righteous servant' *etc.* (*Isa.* 53:11). Those that have the Spirit of Christ have a spirit of self-denial of their own. We see the blessed angels are content to be ministering spirits for us, and it is thought to be the sin of the devil—pride—when he scorned to stoop to the keeping of man, an inferior creature to himself. The blessed angels do not scorn to attend upon a poor child, 'little ones'. A Christian is a consecrated person, and he is none of his own. He is a sacrifice as soon as he is a Christian. He is Christ's. He gives himself to Christ; and as he gives himself, so he gives his life and all to Christ, as Paul says of the Corinthians, they gave themselves and their goods to him (*2 Cor.* 8:5). When a Christian gives himself to Christ, he gives all to Christ; all his labour and pains, and whatsoever he knows that Christ can serve himself of him for his church's good and his glory. He knows that Christ is wiser than he; therefore he resigns himself to his disposal, resolving, if he live, *he lives to the Lord*, and if he die, *he dies to the Lord* (*Rom.* 14:8); that so, whether he live or die, *he may be the Lord's*.

Use 1. Oh, beloved, that we had the spirit of St Paul, and the Spirit of Christ, *to set us a work to do good while we are here*, 'to deny ourselves' (*Titus* 2:12). Oh, it would be meat and drink, as it was to our blessed Saviour Christ, to do good all kinds of ways. Consider all the capacities and abilities we have to do good, this way and that way, in this relation and that relation, that we may be trees of righteousness, that the more we bear the more we may bear. God will mend his own trees. He will purge them and prune them to 'bring forth more fruit' (*John* 15:2). God cherishes fruitful trees. In the law of Moses, when they besieged any place, he commanded them to spare fruitful trees. God spares a fruitful person till he have done his work. We know not how much good one man may do, though he be a mean person. Sometimes one poor wise man delivers the city (*Eccles.* 9:15); and the righteous delivers the land. We see for one servant, Joseph, Potiphar's house was blessed (*Gen.* 39:3). Naaman had a poor maidservant that was the occasion of his conversion (*2 Kings* 5). Grace will set anybody to work. It puts a dexterity into any, though never so mean. They carry God's blessing wheresoever they go, and they bethink themselves when they are in any condition to do good, as he says in Esther 4:14, 'God hath called me to this place, perhaps for end.' We should often put this query to ourselves, Why has God called me to this place? for such and such a purpose?

Now, that we may be fruitful as Paul was, let us labour to have humble spirits.

God delights in an humble spirit, and not in a proud spirit, for that takes all the glory to itself. God delights to use humble spirits, that are content to stoop to any service for others, that think no office too mean.

2. Get *loving* hearts. Love is full of invention, how shall I glorify God? how shall I do good to others? how shall I bring to heaven as many as I can? Love is a sweet and boundless affection, full of holy devices.

3. Labour to have *sufficiency in our places*, that you may have ability to do good. Oh, when these meet together, ability and sufficiency; and a willing, a large, and gracious heart and a fit object to do good to, what a deal of good is done then!

4. And when we find *opportunity of doing any good, let us resolve upon it*, resolve to honour God, and serve him in spite of flesh and blood; for we must get every good

work that we do out of the fire, as it were; we must get it out with travail, and pains. We carry that about us that will hinder us. Let us therefore labour to have sincere aims in that we do to please God, and then resolve to do all the good we can.

To stir us up to be more and more fruitful in our places, let us consider we live for others and not for ourselves, when we are good Christians once. It was a good speech of that godly Palsgrave, great grandfather to him that is Frederick the godly (they called him), when he was to die, *Satis vobis*, said he, *I have lived hitherto for you, now let me live for myself.* We live here all our life for others, therefore let us think while we live, how we may do most good in the church of God.

For encouragement hereunto consider, God will undertake to recompense all the good we do, to a 'cup of cold water' (*Mark* 9:41). We shall not lose a sigh, a groan, for the church. God would account himself dishonoured if it should not be rewarded. He has pawned his faithfulness upon it; 'he is not unfaithful to be unmindful of your good works' (*Heb.* 6:10).

Nay, we have a present reward and contentment of conscience: as light accompanies fire, so peace and joy accompany every good action. All is not reserved for heaven. A Christian has some beginnings of happiness here. When he does that which is contrary to flesh and blood, how full of sweet joy is a fruitful soul! Those that are fruitful in their places never lack arguments of good assurance of salvation. It is your lazy lukewarm Christian that lacks assurance. Therefore I beseech you be stirred up, to live desired in the world, and die lamented; labour to be useful in your places all you can; to be as the olive and fig tree, delighting God and man, and not to cumber the ground of the church with barrenness. Sins of omission,—because men were not fruitful in their places,—was a ground of damnation; 'cast the unprofitable servant into outer darkness' (*Matt.* 25:30); put case he did no harm; aye, but he was *unprofitable*. Such was the cursed disposition of Ephraim; he brought forth fruit to himself (*Hos.* 10:1). Oh this looking to ourselves. When we make ourselves the beginning and the end of all the good we do, it is an argument of a barren person. None ever came to heaven but those that denied themselves.

I see I cannot proceed in this point. You may by the Spirit of God enlarge it in your thoughts and bring home what has been said, to your own souls. Labour that you may be such as others may make use of you, and not be the burdens and calamities of the time, as many are, that live for nothing but to do good men good by vexing of them. That is all the good they do; by vexing their patience they exercise their grace a contrary way.

Let us not be briars and unfruitful plants, labouring to be great by the public miseries. As they say, great fishes grow big by devouring many little ones; as a dragon comes to be great by devouring many little serpents, so many grow great by the ruin of others. Oh beloved, it had been better for such that they had never been born. Therefore as we desire to have comfort when we die, let us labour to be fruitful while we live. St Paul, when the time came that he should die, when he had done his work, you see he that was thus full of self-denial, how gloriously he ended his days. The Second Epistle to Timothy was the last epistle that ever he wrote, and when he had done his work, says he, 'I have fought a good fight, I have kept the faith, I have finished my course: from henceforth there is a crown of righteousness reserved for me' (*2 Tim.* 4:7, 8). What a glorious end is here! and indeed those that are thus careful, and fruitful in their lives and conversations, end their days full of comfort, and resign their souls to God with full assurance of a blessed change, and only those. For you have many, when they come to die, what hinders them? Oh I have been unfruitful, I have not done that good that I might, I have not 'wrought out my salvation with fear and trembling' (*Phil.* 2:12). In such a thing I have done ill, such a thing I have omitted. So they are enemies to their own comfort. Enlarge this in your own meditations, and consider what will comfort you hereafter, when you shall need most comfort. So I leave the text, and come to the occasion.

This holy and blessed man whose funeral now we solemnize, was of St Paul's spirit. He did *desire to die, and be with Christ;* he had a desire while he lived to take all opportunities to do good. I speak of that time when he lived, that is, when he was good, for we live no longer than we are good. Let us not reckon that life wherein we do no good. After God had wrought upon his heart, he had a public heart to do good. If I wanted matter to speak of, I could tell you of his alliance and birth, having two worthy judges of reverend esteem, the one his grandfather, the other his uncle. The one bred him, the other cherished and promoted his study and endeavours; but what should I speak of these things when he has personal worth enough? I need not go abroad to commend this man, for there were those graces and gifts in him that made him so esteemed, that verily, I think, no man of his place and years lived more desired, and died more lamented.

1. For his parts of nature, they were pregnant and solid; but as one said to Melancthon,[8] his disposition and loving mind did gain as much love from men as his parts, though they were great.

2. His learning was good; for beside his own profession, he was a general scholar, and had good skill in that we call elegant learning, and controverted points of divinity. He was a good divine. Indeed, in the turning of his life, when he should

---

[8] Philip Melancthon (1497-1560), friend and colleague of the great German Reformer Martin Luther.

have adventured upon a profession, he had some thoughts of being a divine, had not his friends, especially his uncle, Judge Yelverton, disposed him otherwise, by promoting his study in the law; and when he took upon him that profession, he grew so in it, that he was a credit to the profession for integrity, sincerity, and ability.

3. For his disposition he was every way a man of an excellent sweet temper; mild, and yet resolute; meek, and yet bold where cause was; discreet, yet not over-discreet, so as not to stand out in a good cause in the defence of it; he was humble, yet thought himself too good to be instrumental to any services other than stood with the peace of his conscience; he was tractable and gentle, yet immovably fixed to his principles of piety and honesty; he was exact in his life, yet not censorious;

very conscionable and religious, but without any vain curiosity; indeed, he was every way of a sweet temper. If he stood out in dislike of any, in any matter, he carried it usually with evidence of such sincerity, and denial of self-seeking, that he usually prevailed where he put in.

4. To come to his private personal carriage, it was very pious. He was wont to sequester himself from his employment and labour, to bring his heart under to God, to the guidance of God's Spirit: his study was to study to die; for he gathered choice things out of the sermons he heard about death, many years before he died, to lay up store of provision against that time; and two or three terms before he died he had a special care to inquire of nearer communion with God. He inquired of those he conversed with of the way to attain the same,

and was willing to hear any discourses that tended that way.

5. For his care of the Sabbath, it was his delight. His custom was, after sermon, to retire and ruminate upon what he had heard, to turn it into his spirit. Alas, for want of this, how many sermons are lost in this great city! how much seed is spilt in vain! What nourishment can there be without digestion? it is the second digestion that breeds nourishment; when we chew things, and call them to mind again, and make them our own. This was his custom every Sabbath.

6. For his carriage to others, he was a constant friend, and his study was, to labour to make those good he conversed withal. He conversed with few, but they were the better for him, he was so fruitful; and he would have intimate society with

none, but he would do good or take good from them. You have many in the society where he lived that may bless God all the days of their life that ever they knew him.

7. For his carriage in his government of the place where he lived, I think there are none that are able to judge, but will give him the testimony of a faithful, prudent governor. He was so careful of the town where he was recorder, that he provided for them after his death, and gave them a large legacy, two hundred merks, to set the poor on work.

8. For the honourable society wherein he was a governor, he carried himself with that resolution, for good order and good exercises, and was such a strict opposer of any abuse, which he judged to be so, that the house will have a special want of him, I fear: rather, I desire from my soul, that that

honourable society may so flourish as they may have no want of good Master Sherland.

9. For his more public carriage, by virtue of his place at Northampton, where he was recorder, he was called to be a member of the body-representative in Parliament, wherein both his ability and spirit appeared to all that knew him. You may see by this what manner of man we have lost.

He died before he was come to the middle of his years, a young man to speak of; and he did a great deal of work in a little time. God had ripened him for his business extraordinarily, and gave him a spirit to bestir himself to do all the good he could. These be wondrous ill times, beloved, to lose such men as he was; therefore we have cause to lay it to heart the more. The commonwealth wants him, the town and country where he lived will want him, the society where he was a governor will want him, the family where he was a governor will find a miss in him. He went wisely in and out; he was able for family duties; he had more than ordinary sufficiency; he was of Joshua's mind, 'Choose who you will serve, but I and my house will serve the Lord' (*Josh.* 24:15); and to help him the more, he had the happiness to marry into a religious family; he had a good helper.

Now for the church. Though his profession was the law, yet that will have a great want of him. He was a hearty and true promoter of the cause of religion, and showed his love to the church, by his care of it now he is departed. He gave four hundred pounds to buy in impropriations; he gave an hundred pounds for the breeding up of poor scholars, and there is never a good minister round about where he lived, but had encouragement from him. Indeed, he was a man of special use and service; and as he honoured God in his life, so God has honoured him in his death, as you may see by this honourable assembly of worthy people, met in love to him.

His death was, as the death of strong men use to be, with conflicts between nature and his disease, but with a great deal of patience; and in his sickness time he would utter Paul's disposition, Oh, said he, you keep me from heaven, you keep me from glory, being displeased with those that kept him alive, with conference out of love.

He had a large heart to do good, for though he were fruitful, and studied to be fruitful, yet oft in his sickness in a complaining manner he would say, Oh, I have not been so wise for my own soul as I ought to be; I have not been provident enough in taking opportunities of doing and receiving good.

Beloved, shall such a man as he was, so careful, so fruitful, so good, shall he complain thus? What shall a company of us do? Beloved, those that have warmed their hearts at the fire of God's love, they think zeal itself to be coldness, and fruitfulness to be barrenness. Love is a boundless affection. He spoke not this from want of care; but love knows no bounds. Therefore he took the more opportunities of doing good.

Well, I beseech you, beloved, let not this example pass without making good use of it. God will call us to a reckoning, not only for what we hear, but for what we see: he will call us to a reckoning for the examples of his people. Therefore, as we see here what a holy disposition was in St Paul, and in this blessed man now with God, so let us labour to find the same disposition in ourselves. Paul has now his desire; he is dissolved and he is with Christ, that is best of all. This holy man has his desire; he desired not to be kept from his glory and happiness, on which his mind was set before. Let us therefore labour with God in the use of good means, to have the same disposition; and in this moment let us provide for eternity; out of eternity before, and eternity after, issues this little spot of time to do good in. Let us sow to the Spirit, account all time lost that either we do not or take not, good in. Opportunity is God's angel. Time is short, but opportunity is shorter. Let us catch at all opportunities. This is the time of worship. Oh, let us sow now. Shall we go to sowing then, when the time comes that we should reap? Some begin to sow when they die, that is the reaping time. While we have time let us do all good, especially where God loves most, to those that are good.

Consider the standings and places that God has set us in; consider the advantages in our hands, the price that we have; consider that opportunity will not stay long. Let us therefore do all the good we can, and so if we do, beloved, we shall come at length to reap that, that this blessed saint of God, St Paul here in the text, and this blessed man, for whose cause we are now met, do enjoy. Therefore, if we desire to end our days in joy and comfort, let us lay the foundation of a comfortable death now often. To die well is not a thing of that light moment as some imagine: it is no easy matter. But to die well is a matter of every day. Let us daily do some good that may help us at the time of our death. Every day by repentance pull out the sting of some sin, that so when death comes, we may have nothing to do but to die. To die well is the action of the whole life. He never dies well for the most part that dies not daily, as Paul says of himself, 'I die daily' (*1 Cor.* 15:31); he laboured to loose his heart from the world, and worldly things. If we loose our hearts from the world and die daily, how easy will it be to die at last! He that thinks of the vanity of the world, and of death, and of being with Christ for ever, and is dying daily, it will be easy for him to end his days with comfort. But the time being past, I will here make an end. Let us desire God to make that which has been spoken effectual, both concerning Paul, and likewise concerning this blessed man, for whose cause we are met together.

RICHARD SIBBES
(1577-1635)

Richard Sibbes—the 'heavenly Doctor' as he came to be called—was a man who clearly enjoyed knowing God. And even centuries later, his relish is infectious. He spoke of the living God as a life-giving, warming sun who 'delights to spread his beams and his influence in inferior things, to make all things fruitful. Such a goodness is in God as is in a fountain, or in the breast that loves to ease itself of milk.'

And knowing God to be such an over-flowing fountain of goodness and love made him a most attractive model of God-likeness. For, he said, 'those that are led with the Spirit of God, that are like him; they have a communicative, diffusive goodness that loves to spread itself'. In other words, knowing God's love, he became loving; and his understanding of who God is transformed him into a man, a preacher, and a writer of magnetic geniality. He was never married, but looking at his life, it is clear that he had a quite extraordinary ability for cultivating warm and lasting friendships. Charles Spurgeon once told his students that he loved the sort of minister whose face invites you to be his friend, the sort of face on which you read the sign 'Welcome' and not 'Beware of the dog.' He could have been describing Sibbes.

Sibbes was born to a wheelwright in a rather obscure little village in Suffolk. Few could have expected how influential young Sibbes would turn out to be. Before long, though, it was clear that he was remarkably capable: sailing through his studies at Cambridge, he became a tutor at St John's College aged only twenty-four. Bright as he was, though, it was his ability as a preacher that soon began to mark him out. Before long, he was appointed to be a 'lecturer' at Holy Trinity Church in Cambridge (where a gallery had to be built to accommodate the extra numbers he attracted), and a few years later he was appointed to be a preacher at Gray's Inn, one of the London Inns of Court where many soon-to-be-influential men of Puritan persuasion came to hear him.

Knowing, as he once said, that there is

more grace in Christ than there is sin in us, he always sought in his preaching to win the hearts of his listeners to Christ. This, he believed, was the special duty of ministers: 'they woo for Christ, and open the riches, beauty, honour, and all that is lovely in him.' The result was preaching so winsome that struggling believers began to call him the 'honey-mouthed', the 'sweet dropper', and, apparently, hardened sinners deliberately avoided his sermons for fear he would convert them. One listener, Humphrey Mills, recorded his experience of Sibbes's ministry, and it seems to have been typical:

> I was for three years together wounded for sins, and under a sense of my corruptions, which were many; and I followed sermons, pursuing the means, and was constant in duties and doing; looking for Heaven that way. And then

I was so precise for outward formalities, that I censured all to be reprobates, that wore their hair anything long, and not short above their ears; or that wore great ruffs, and gorgets, or fashions, and follies. But yet I was distracted in my mind, wounded in conscience, and wept often and bitterly, and prayed earnestly, but yet had no comfort, till I heard that sweet saint . . . Doctor Sibbs, by whose means and ministry I was brought to peace and joy in my spirit. His sweet soul-melting Gospel-sermons won my heart and refreshed me much, for by him I saw and had much of God and was confident in Christ, and could overlook the world . . . my heart held firm and resolved and my desires all heaven-ward.

In 1626, Sibbes was appointed Master of Katharine Hall, Cambridge, and for the last decade of his life he would use his considerable influence to promote his Christ-centred theology. He sought to place trusted Puritan preachers in church teaching posts around the country; he personally nurtured a number of young ministers, men such as Thomas Goodwin, John Cotton, Jeremiah Burroughs, John Preston, and Philip Nye; and through his printed sermons he affected countless more.

Richard Sibbes is, in my opinion, the best introduction to the Puritans. Ever since the day when, as a student, I read his *The Bruised Reed*, Sibbes has been my favourite. 'Sibbes never wastes the student's time', wrote Spurgeon, 'he scatters pearls and diamonds with both hands.' Reading him is like sitting in the sunshine: he gets into your heart and warms it to Christ.

MICHAEL REEVES

THE BANNER OF TRUTH TRUST

3 Murrayfield Road,
Edinburgh EH12 6EL,
UK

PO Box 621, Carlisle,
PA 17013,
USA

www.banneroftruth.co.uk